FINDING OUT ABOUT
WATER ANIMALS

Published by
Oxford University Press, Walton Street, Oxford OX2 6DP
Oxford New York Toronto Delhi Bombay Calcutta Madras
Karachi Petaling Jaya Singapore Hong Kong Tokyo Nairobi
Dar es Salaam Cape Town Melbourne Auckland

ISBN 0 19 918227 2

Typesetting by Thomas/Weintroub Associates, London
Colour separations by Trilogy, Milan
Printed in Italy

Created and produced by Ilex Publishers Ltd.,
29-31 George Street, Oxford OX1 2AJ, in association
with Linden Artists Ltd., 86 Petty France, London SW1H 9EA.

Illustrated by Martin Camm/Linden Artists

FINDING OUT ABOUT
WATER ANIMALS

Written by Mark Carwardine
Illustrated by Martin Camm

Oxford University Press

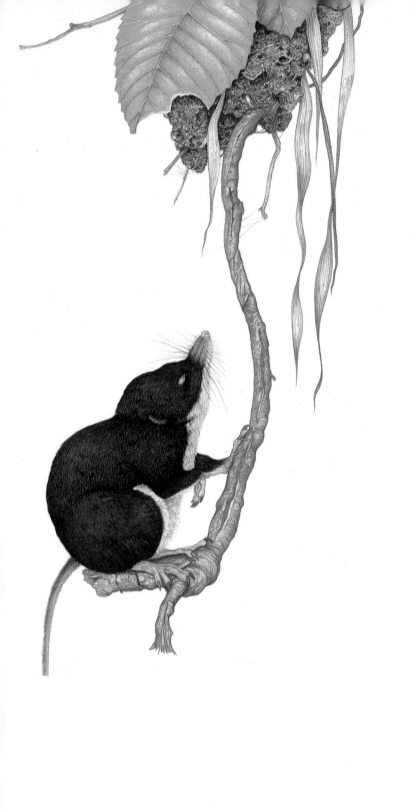

CONTENTS

Grizzly bear

Grizzly bears are very fond of eating. They will sometimes eat more than eight large salmon before feeling full. First-class salmon fishermen, they leap into the water with a splash and pin the unfortunate fish onto the bottom. They also feed on berries, insects, mice and voles, young deer, the remains of dead animals, and even the leftovers from people's picnics.

Grizzlies are so-called because their coats look grizzled – or streaked with grey – not because they are bad-tempered. However, they can be very dangerous and, since they are unable to see very well, often mistake people for bears. When they feel threatened or annoyed they fight, using their famous 'bear hugs' or strong teeth and claws. They can charge at fifty kilometres an hour and, when standing on two legs, are much taller than a man – and certainly much stronger.

Grizzlies, or brown bears as they are often called, live in Alaska, Canada and Russia. Very small numbers are also found in Europe and northern Asia. But almost everywhere they are much rarer than they used to be because of hunting and other threats to their survival.

Grizzly bears are born inside caves and hollow trees, between January and March. They remain hidden in these dens until spring or early summer, before venturing outside for the first time. Even then, they prefer to stay with their mothers for another four years or more before looking after themselves.

Marine iguana

Along the beautiful shores of the Galapagos Islands, many miles off the coast of South America, thousands of giant lizards lie out on the rocks to sunbathe. Known as marine iguanas, they spend every day warming themselves in the sun.

Although almost two metres long, they are completely harmless creatures, feeding on seaweed and other water plants. They are the only lizards in the world that like to live in the sea.

The iguanas hide in rock crevices during the night, but wander out at dawn as soon as the sun begins to rise. When they have warmed up they dive into the sea to find something to eat. They happily swim underwater — moving with a snake-like

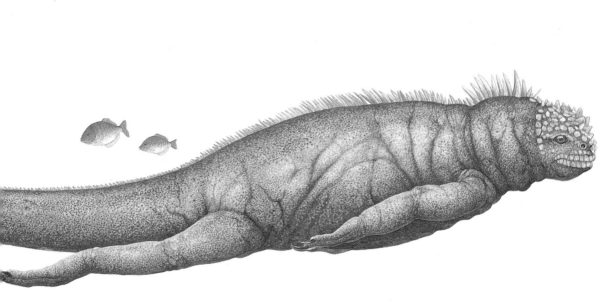

motion – rather than
paddling their legs.
Occasionally, they haul out
onto a rock, clinging on
against the strength of the
waves with their long,
powerful claws.

During the breeding
season, the male iguanas
often fight over females.
They butt their heads
together and try to push one
another out of the way. But
for the rest of the year they
seem to be the best of
friends, sunbathing side-by-
side and even lying on top of
one another.

Otter civet

Thirsty birds and other small animals visiting a stream or swamp to drink, in parts of south-east Asia, have to be very careful. Quietly hiding in the water, with only the tip of its nose showing above the surface, may be an otter civet waiting to pounce.

Otter civets live in Vietnam, Malaysia, Sumatra and Borneo, usually near rivers, swamps and streams. As well as birds, they feed on a variety of small animals including frogs, snails, fish, mice and crabs. They also sometimes eat fruit and other plants.

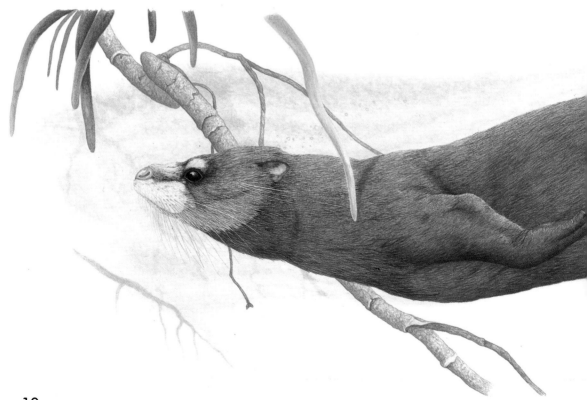

Just over half a metre long and with slightly webbed feet, they look rather like the otters after which they are named. However, they are comparatively slow swimmers and spend much more time out of the water than most otters. They can even climb very well and often choose to hide in trees, rather than in the water, when they are being chased.

Unmistakable with such remarkably long whiskers and a short tail, the otter civet's most unusual feature is the shape of its face. It appears to have padding inside its upper lips – though, of course, it doesn't – making them stick out at the sides.

Amazon river dolphin

Amazon river dolphins are very friendly animals. They often come to the aid of injured or troubled companions, even risking danger themselves. They have been seen swimming arm-in-arm, a healthy dolphin on either side of an injured one, regularly carrying it to the surface to breathe.

Little more than two metres long, Amazon river dolphins are very brightly-coloured compared with most other members of the dolphin family. The older they are the pinker they become.

In some parts of the Amazon Basin, where they live, they even help the local people. They come to the call of the fishermen, herding fish from deeper water to their nets in the shallows.

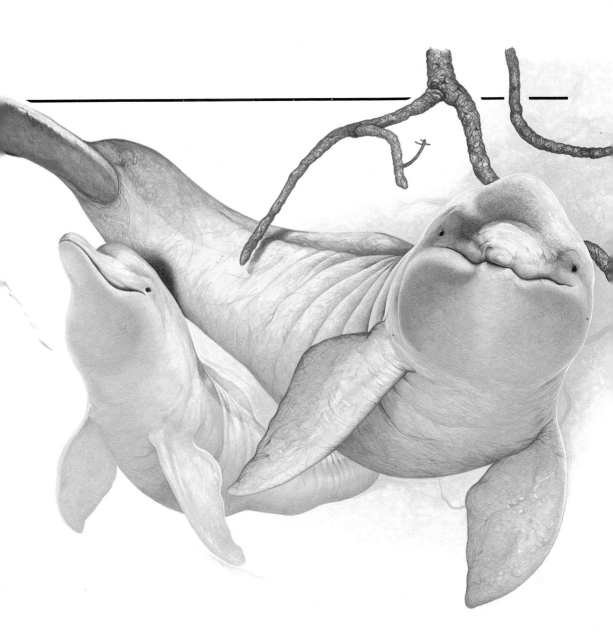

They often live in pairs, hunting together for fish, and sometimes crabs and shrimps, which they swallow whole. Baby river dolphins, or calves, are thought to be born between July and September. They are almost half as long as their parents but continue to grow for many years. Like their parents, they have very poor eyesight. They use a form of echolocation – like bats – to find their way around and to catch food.

Narwhal

The narwhal only has two teeth. In the male, one of these grows so big that it sticks out through his upper lip and forms a spiralling tusk. Such tusks have been known to grow to three metres long.

No-one really knows what the narwhal's tusk is for. It might be used to break through ice on the surface of the sea; or to skewer prey; or even to probe along the bottom of the sea for food. However, it is most likely to be used as a weapon. Narwhals have been seen using them like swords, fencing together on the ocean surface. This may be quite common, as many of the animals have nasty scars — and one was even seen with a broken tusk sticking out of its head.

Narwhals are relatives of the whales and dolphins. They live in the cold waters of the Arctic, particularly between northern Canada and Greenland, where they feed on fish, shrimps, squid, octopus and other ocean animals. Able to dive to three hundred and seventy metres or more, and to stay underwater for as long as fifteen minutes, they like the sea to be very deep. However, they often swim into shallow estuaries and fjords in the summer to have their young. Their calves, which are about a third the size of the parents when they are first born, will eventually grow to a length of four or five metres.

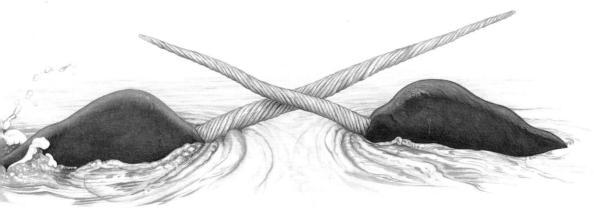

Californian sealion

Californian sealions are so playful that sometimes they chase and catch their own air bubbles underwater. They are also very intelligent and have a good memory, making them popular animals in circuses. Indeed, they are probably best known for balancing balls on their noses, clapping with their flippers and blowing circus trumpets.

In the wild, they often play together by leaping from the water and diving back in headfirst. Groups of up to twenty young sealions will swim along in single file and perform this favourite trick one after the other.

There are several different kinds of sealion, living in many parts of the world, but the Californian variety is found only in the Pacific Ocean.

About twenty metres long, it lives along the coast and islands of western North America, particularly in California and Mexico. It also occurs further south, in the Galapagos Islands, where it is known as the Galapagos sealion.

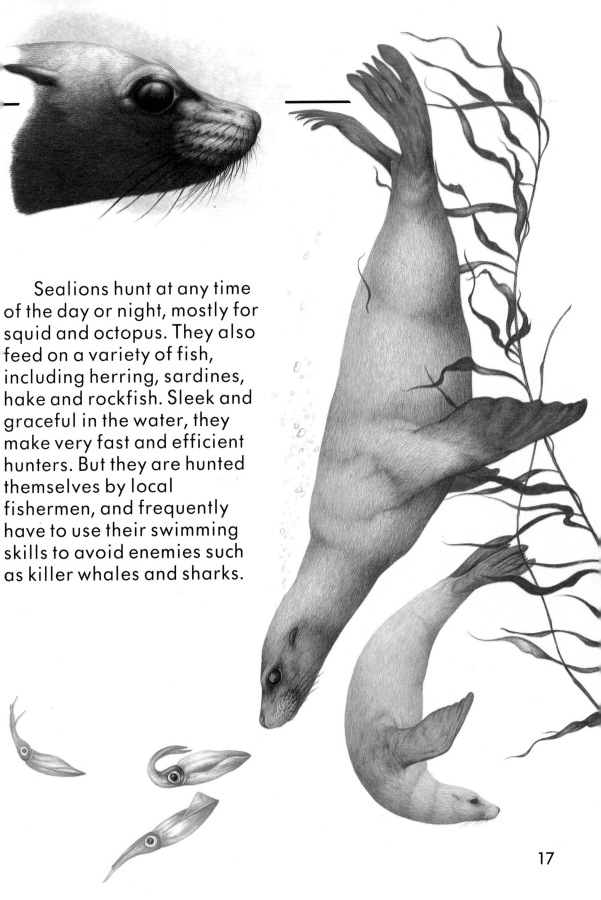

Sealions hunt at any time of the day or night, mostly for squid and octopus. They also feed on a variety of fish, including herring, sardines, hake and rockfish. Sleek and graceful in the water, they make very fast and efficient hunters. But they are hunted themselves by local fishermen, and frequently have to use their swimming skills to avoid enemies such as killer whales and sharks.

Gharial

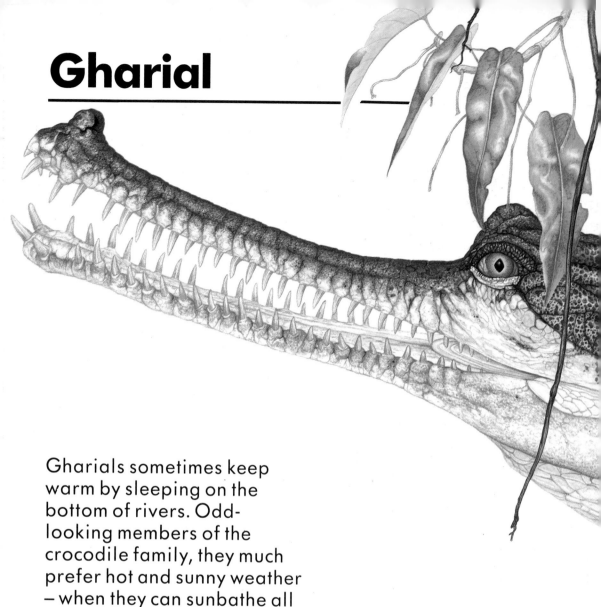

Gharials sometimes keep warm by sleeping on the bottom of rivers. Odd-looking members of the crocodile family, they much prefer hot and sunny weather – when they can sunbathe all day long – to cold winds and rain.

They were once very common animals in rivers all over India, Nepal, Pakistan and Bangladesh. But so many of them were killed by hunters that, ten years ago, only about sixty were still alive.

Special sanctuaries were therefore set up – where they could live in safety – and their numbers have slowly increased once again. There are now several thousand of them in the wild.

Gharials dig holes in the ground in which to lay their eggs. These are usually no more than a few metres from the water's edge, as the animals find it very difficult to move on land. When laying is complete, the females carefully cover the eggs with soil and return to the river. From a safe distance they quietly watch the nests, to make sure their eggs are not stolen by mongooses, lizards or people, before they hatch.

Gharials grow up to about six metres long, though the females are generally much smaller. They feed on fish (which are caught at night) using their special piercing teeth to keep a tight hold on the slippery prey. Each gharial has more than a hundred teeth in its slender mouth for this purpose.

Galapagos penguin

Penguins are best-known for living in the freezing cold Antarctic. But Galapagos penguins are unusual because they live on the equator. About ten thousand of them breed in two areas of the Galapagos Islands.

One of the rarest of the world's sixteen different penguins, the Galapagos penguin stands only about half a metre tall and is also one of the smallest. Like others of its kind it cannot fly – but has special wings – which have become strong flippers. These are used to 'fly' through water instead, making them among the best swimmers and divers in the bird world.

Galapagos penguins spend as much as twelve hours every day hunting for fish in the sea. Although they live in the tropics – and it can get very hot on land – the water around their island home is very cold. So the penguins have three layers of feathers and plenty of fat to keep them warm.

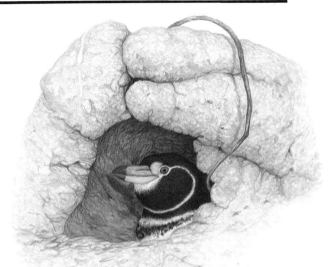

This means, however, that when they are on the land they have to keep out of the sun as much as possible to avoid overheating.

Unlike many other penguins, which breed in enormous colonies, the Galapagos penguins prefer to be in pairs or small groups.

They lay their eggs in caves or caverns close to the sea – so if it gets too hot, they can simply dive into the water for a few minutes to cool off.

White pelican

Pelicans never use their enormous pouches to store fish, as many people wrongly believe. Instead, they use them as nets to catch the fish underwater.

They dive into the water or work in 'fishing schools' where they sit on the surface together and surround and trap shoals of fish, then submerge their heads and

necks to scoop up the prey. They all do this at exactly the same time, giving the appearance of performing a well-rehearsed dance routine.

White pelicans are found in many parts of the world, including Africa, south-east Europe, south-west Russia and parts of western Asia. Like all pelicans, they are good fliers – travelling in V-formation – and often commute hundreds of kilometres from their nests to the best fishing lakes.

They always breed in groups, or colonies, on the ground. The males gather the nesting material and the females build the nests. Several eggs are laid but usually only one – very noisy – baby survives.

White pelicans are quite common birds, often living in colonies numbering forty thousand or more. But some kinds are now very rare. Indeed the Dalmation pelican, which is the rarest of all, may have as few as a thousand survivors left.

Blue whale

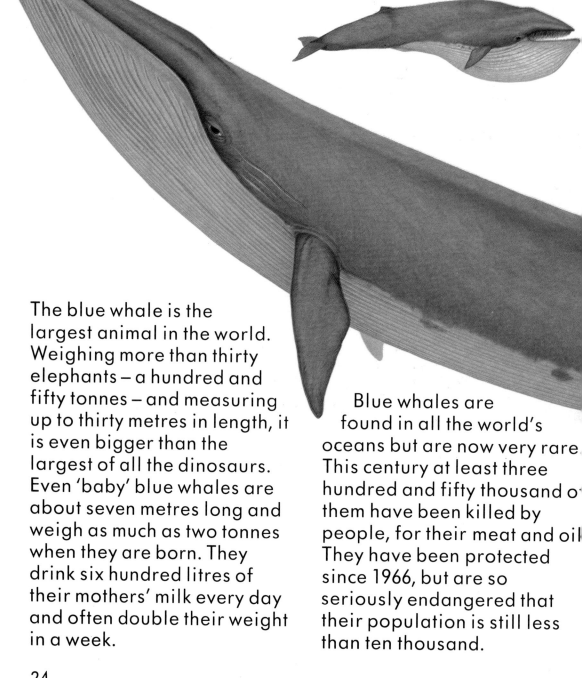

The blue whale is the largest animal in the world. Weighing more than thirty elephants – a hundred and fifty tonnes – and measuring up to thirty metres in length, it is even bigger than the largest of all the dinosaurs. Even 'baby' blue whales are about seven metres long and weigh as much as two tonnes when they are born. They drink six hundred litres of their mothers' milk every day and often double their weight in a week.

Blue whales are found in all the world's oceans but are now very rare. This century at least three hundred and fifty thousand of them have been killed by people, for their meat and oil. They have been protected since 1966, but are so seriously endangered that their population is still less than ten thousand.

Despite their enormous size, blue whales feed entirely on tiny shrimp-like animals, called krill. These are less than five centimetres long – so the whales have to eat enormous numbers of them – probably as many as forty million every day. But they only feed during the summer months, preferring not to eat at all for about eight months of the year.

Blue whales are mammals – not fish – so they have to come to the surface to breathe about every quarter of an hour. For this reason they cannot stay underwater and sleep for too long, otherwise they would drown. When they rise to the surface they breathe out through their blowholes, spouting water over nine metres into the air, before breathing in and diving once again.

Moose

Moose normally walk very carefully and quietly through the undergrowth of their woodland homes. If they stumble upon hunters – and can see no means of escape – they will even try to hide behind a tree rather than run. But if there is a chance that they haven't been seen, they risk running away as fast as they can. Some individuals have been known to exceed fifty kilometres an hour in their attempts to escape.

Moose, or elk as they are sometimes called, are the largest deer in the world. They are unmistakable animals, with their massive antlers, and sometimes stand over two metres high at the shoulders. Once found in many parts of Europe, and all over the United States and Canada, they have been wiped out by hunters in some regions. However, they are still common in many places and continue to be hunted for sport.

Moose are most active at dusk and dawn, but can be seen almost any time during the day. They are particularly fond of marshy regions and will paddle in the water for hours on end.

Water plants are among their favourite foods and they sometimes disappear under the surface in their eagerness to find them. They also feed on twigs and the bark of trees, and on many other plants. A particularly hungry moose will eat over a thousand plants in a single day.

Torrent duck

In the rivers of the Andes, in South America, an amazing bird spends most of its life battling against the fast-flowing currents. It dives off boulders into the water and completely disappears underneath; or it fights its way upstream, for half an hour or more, swimming with just its head poking out above the surface. Sometimes it gives up, lets go and shoots back down the river with the current, bouncing and bobbing as it goes.

This remarkable and striking bird is a torrent duck.

The male has a stunning white head streaked with black; the female a beautiful reddish face and breast.

Perfectly adapted for swimming in the swirling whitewaters, the torrent duck has a very streamlined shape and a long stiff tail for steering. Its webbed feet are so enormous that torrent duck eggs have to be specially big for them to fit inside, before hatching. The feet are usually used for swimming – but they also come in useful if the bird wants to run across the water – when it is in a hurry.

They even have sharp claws for gripping onto slippery surfaces. These help the duck to keep a foothold on a submerged rock, when it is resting and the water is swirling around its legs.

Torrent ducks feed only on the larvae of stoneflies, which live among the underwater weeds of their river homes. As a result, they never venture too far away and rarely need to fly.

Duck-billed platypus

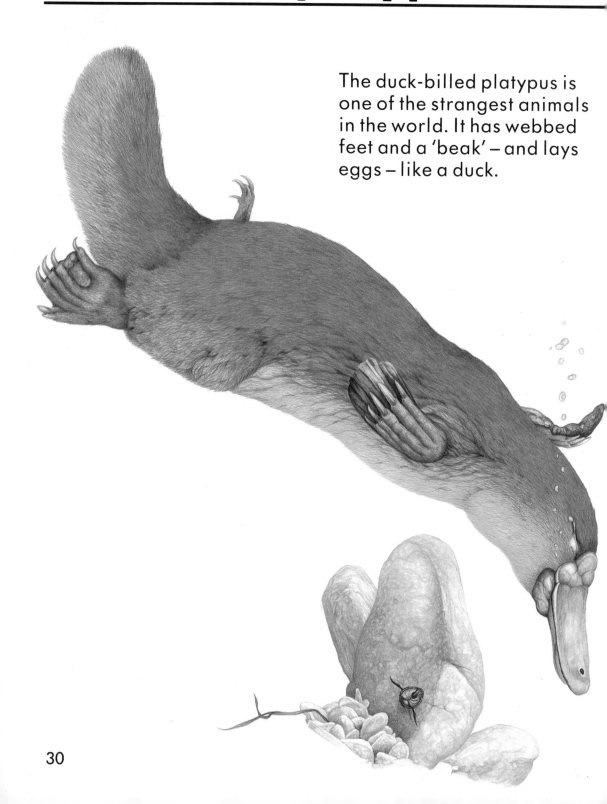

The duck-billed platypus is one of the strangest animals in the world. It has webbed feet and a 'beak' – and lays eggs – like a duck.

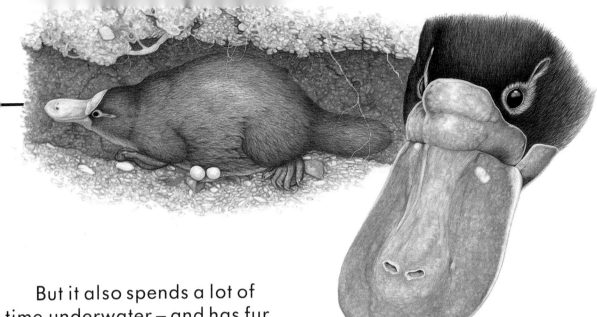

But it also spends a lot of time underwater – and has fur and a flat tail – like a beaver.

Found in eastern Australia and Tasmania, the platypus lives in freshwater streams, rivers, lakes and lagoons. It is a small animal, about sixty centimetres long from the tip of its soft leathery snout to the end of its tail.

Platypuses find walking on land really difficult, but are very graceful creatures in the water. This is where they find worms, shellfish, insects and other water animals to eat. They hunt using their sensitive bills, or snouts, because when diving they close their eyes and ears, so cannot see or hear a thing. As soon as they have collected enough food together they carry it up to the surface, in their cheek pouches, to chew and swallow.

Platypuses live in burrows – up to eighty metres long – in the banks of rivers and streams. During the breeding season, they build special burrows, with bedrooms at the end, in which to lay their two or three tiny, soft eggs. These hatch after about ten days, but the babies remain safely hidden underground for another three or four months before venturing into the outside world.

Shark

The shark is probably the most feared animal in the world. With its streamlined body, needle-sharp teeth, glaring eyes and a nose that can smell food from miles away, it has a terrible reputation.

But not all sharks are dangerous. Some are barely fifteen centimetres long and would be incapable of causing much harm. Two of the world's biggest – the fifteen-metre long whale shark and the ten-metre long basking shark – both eat tiny animals called plankton and are also completely harmless. Most other kinds eat fish. Even the so-called man-eating shark will often swim past people without attacking.

But it is true that some, like the hammerhead and great white sharks, can be very dangerous. To a six-metre long great white shark, with teeth the length of a finger, a fully-grown man would make a very tasty snack.

No-one knows for sure how often these and other sharks injure or kill people.

About fifty attacks are reported from around the world every year; as many as a thousand more probably go unrecorded. Even so, the chances of any one person actually being attacked – or even seeing a shark – while swimming in the sea are very small indeed.

Manatee

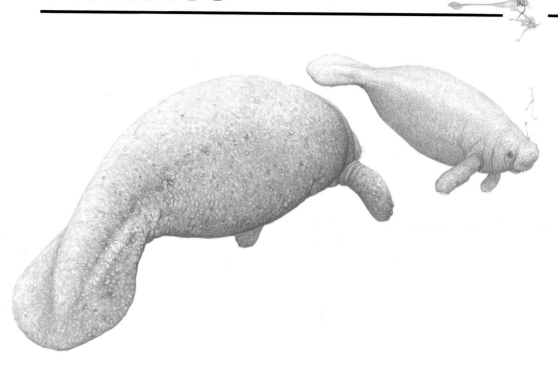

Manatees are really underwater cows. They live in the bays, estuaries, rivers and shallow coastal waters of some of the warmer parts of America and Africa.

Unfortunately, their eyesight is not very good and, in murky water, they keep bumping into things. They are supposed to graze only on water grasses and other plants – which is why they are nicknamed 'sea cows' or 'fish cows' – but they occasionally eat small fish by mistake, for the same reason.

Many manatees have been killed by hunters and they are now quite rare. But they are friendly animals, often playing together or kissing when they meet. Normally quiet, they spend hours peacefully resting with their eyes closed, but squeal, chirp and scream when they are frightened or annoyed.

Manatees are excellent swimmers, able to stay underwater for up to a quarter of an hour, and can reach speeds of up to twenty-five kilometres per hour or more.

They use their flattened tails as paddles and sometimes 'walk' along the bottom on their flippers.

The calves are born underwater. Immediately, they are helped to the surface by their mothers, to breathe for the first time. Within an hour they are able to swim around on their own.

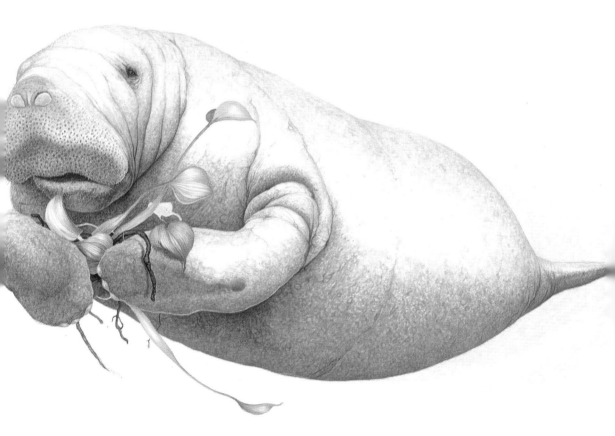

Water shrew

When it is swimming, the water shrew uses the air trapped in its fur like a rubber ring to help it float. This works perfectly when the shrew wants to swim along the surface – but makes diving and staying underwater very difficult. The best it can manage is about twenty seconds before floating back up.

When it has been for a swim, the water shrew likes to wring itself dry by squeezing into a narrow tunnel, which it digs itself into the side of a bank.

Water shrews live near streams, rivers and ponds in many parts of the world. They particularly like watercress beds and, in Scotland, prefer rocky beaches. But despite their name they also spend a lot of time out of the water and, particularly in northern Europe, can be seen in woodland and forests.

Water shrews only live for about one and a half years. In order to fit everything into such short lives, they always seem to be in a hurry.

Constantly busy and on the move, they are active at night and during the day, snatching just a little sleep whenever they get the chance.

Only about ten centimetres long, the shrews often feed on animals much bigger than themselves. Their prey includes insects, fish and frogs, which they nearly always attack from behind. They also have a poisonous bite, which helps to weaken the unsuspecting animals before they are killed and eaten.

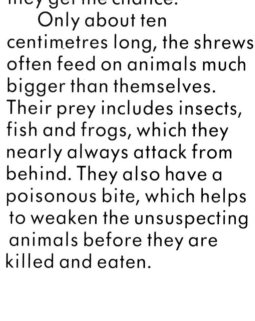

37

Bearded seal

The bearded seal is easily recognised by its long whiskers, which look rather like a moustache. A very common animal, it lives in the cold waters of the Arctic and sub-arctic.

Although fairly big animals, almost three metres long, bearded seals get frightened very easily. They are as curious as a cat – and interested in anything unusual – but as soon as there is the slightest sign of danger they become almost paralyzed with fear. Even when they are out of the sea, resting on land or ice, they always lie with their heads very close to the water ready for a quick escape.

But they do have good reason for being nervous. They live alone for most of the year – and are often hunted by polar bears, killer whales and eskimos – so can never really relax and must always keep a wary eye open for danger.

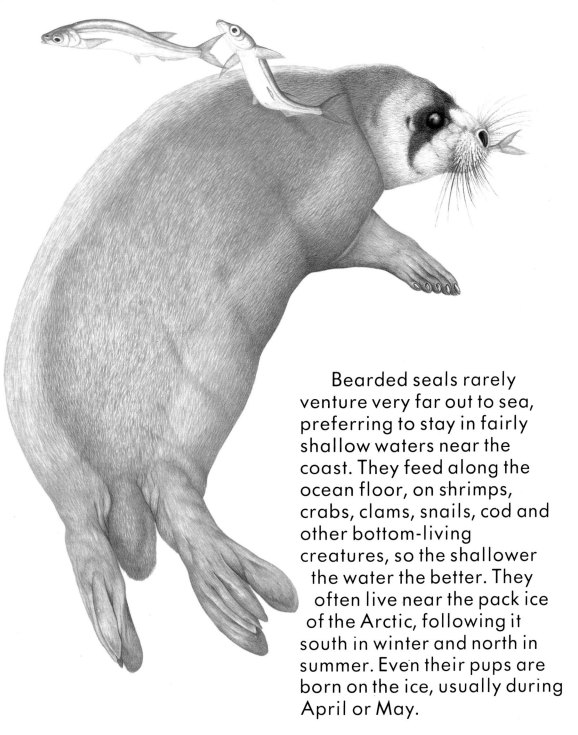

Bearded seals rarely venture very far out to sea, preferring to stay in fairly shallow waters near the coast. They feed along the ocean floor, on shrimps, crabs, clams, snails, cod and other bottom-living creatures, so the shallower the water the better. They often live near the pack ice of the Arctic, following it south in winter and north in summer. Even their pups are born on the ice, usually during April or May.

Malayan tapir

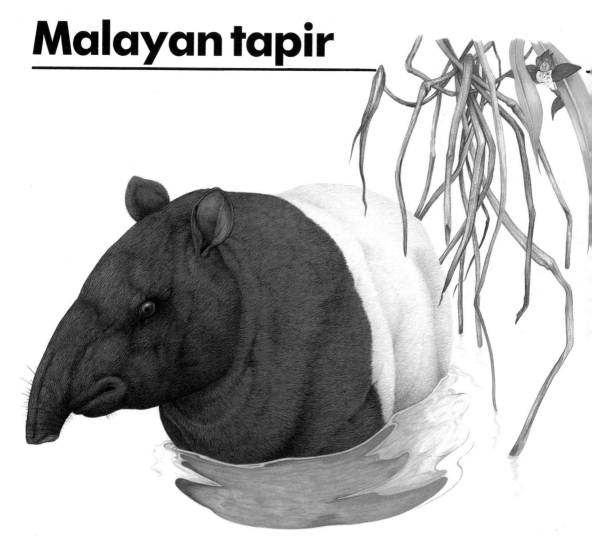

In parts of south-east Asia a curious-looking animal can sometimes be seen walking through the jungle with its long nose close to the ground. It is a very rare Malayan tapir, carefully sniffing its path to make sure it hasn't got lost.

The tapir also uses its nose as an extra finger, to pull food within easy reach of its mouth. It feeds on grasses, water plants, soft twigs, leaves, buds, fruits and green shoots. These are mostly eaten at night, in forest clearings and along river banks.

The spectacular black-and-white colouring of the Malayan tapir makes it very difficult to see in the dark.

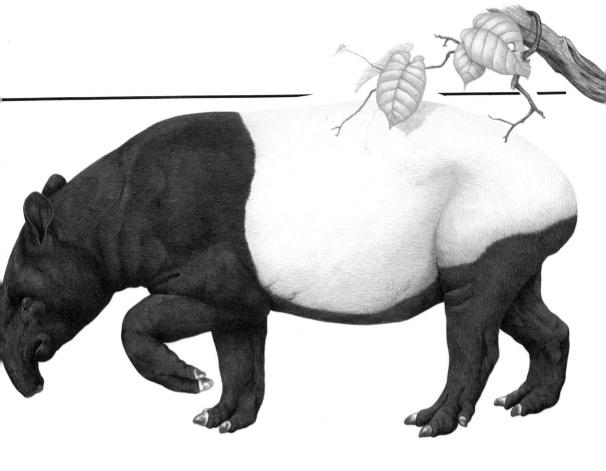

There is a legend which says it was once completely black – but had a white blanket over its back to keep warm – and, as a result, it is still sometimes called the blanket tapir.

In real life, however, tapirs spend a great deal of their time trying to keep cool. They are excellent swimmers and often lounge around in water during the heat of the day. They have even been seen holding their breath and walking along the bottom of rivers, just like hippos.

Baby tapirs look quite different to their parents. They have brown coats, dappled with white spots and stripes, which provide good camouflage when they are hiding in jungle undergrowth. By the time they are six months old, however, they have grown the black-and-white coats of their parents.

Sea otter

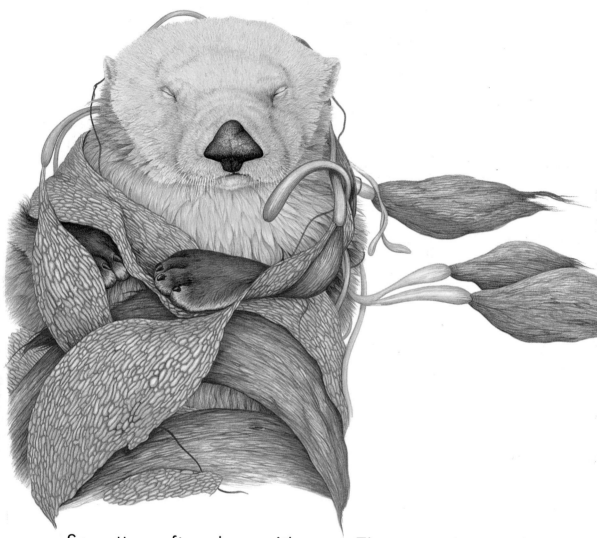

Sea otters often sleep with their paws over their eyes. Lying in the water, they also tie themselves to giant seaweed to avoid drifting out to sea during the night.

They spend most of their lives in the water, though never so far out that they might lose sight of the coast. The only times they climb out of the sea are during particularly bad storms.

Sea otters live along the rocky coasts of the North Pacific, in western North America and eastern Russia. They are excellent swimmers, paddling along with their hind legs and using their tails as oars, and can dive to depths of up to forty metres. On the seabed they search for crabs, mussels, fish, snails, sea urchins and other animals, catching the prey with their front paws. They then swim to the surface to eat, cracking open the shells with a stone and using their chests as tables while floating on their backs. When they have finished, they simply roll over to wash the bits of shell and leftover food from their fur.

Baby otters are born in the water and ride on their mothers' chests for six or seven weeks. Then they begin taking lessons in swimming, diving and catching food. These last for as long as six months, until the babies are able to look after themselves.

Common dolphin

Common dolphins can dive as deep as two hundred and eighty metres and can stay underwater for as long as eight minutes. Sleek and streamlined, they are excellent swimmers and often leap into the air just for fun.

They are very intelligent and friendly animals, enjoying the company of others and living in large groups, or 'schools'. Normally there are between about twenty and a few hundred dolphins in a typical school – but one seen in New Zealand was a solid mass of them measuring twenty-seven kilometres wide and forty-four kilometres long!

Common dolphins are a little over two metres in length. They have beautiful patterns on their bodies, which make them very hard to see in the dappled light near the surface.

They feed on fish such as sardines, anchovy and herring, and sometimes eat crabs. Some individuals have even been seen catching flying fish in mid-air.

Common dolphins have been hunted for many years but, fortunately, are still fairly common. They are found in oceans and coastal waters all over the world, from Iceland to South America.